A Dance with the Sunflowers

by Lucia Cecilia Hope

Dedicated to Mum and Papa, who have raised me with the most incredible love, sacrifice and compassion, and to my siblings, without whose support I could never be the person I am today. How blessed I am to have a family who loves my craziness.

Introduction

To say I am not proud of this mis-matched collection of verses would be a lie. Yet to say I am proud would be a lie also. No, "proud" is not the right word… "relieved", perhaps? Or "nervous"? Although maybe these adjectives contradict one another, I believe both are true. It is relieving to spill my thoughts out with pen and paper and lay them open for all to see. I am relieved that people may pick up this book, may venture to give it a chance, and may find a little glimpse of their own soul hidden in the ink. And yet, I am nervous. Nervous for those flicking through these pages to see such vulnerability, such rawness, such exposure. I am nervous to dare publish my amateur scrawl alongside poets who have sculpted timeless classics from the same words I use. But then again, where would we be in life if we dared not expose ourselves? I do not claim perfection in this book- on the contrary, I wish to draw light on the many faults and imperfections you may find here. But don't, I beg, take this as an expression of false humility or of arrogance. Rather, I wish for you to read these ramblings of my mind, notice their faults, and yet love the unguarded manner in which I have expressed them. Take from the verses what you will- I hope only for you to embrace the paradox of perfect imperfection which only human souls have fortune enough to accomplish.

Chapters

I. Early Works --------------------------------------- 3

    o The Virtues ------------------------------ 4
    o BANG ------------------------------------- 5
    o My Boy ----------------------------------- 6
    o The House on Mill Street Corner ----------- 7

II. Prose and Posies --------------------------------- 8

    o Outcast ---------------------------------- 9
    o What Life Can Be ------------------------- 11
    o Quite Beautiful -------------------------- 12
    o Daydreamer ------------------------------- 13
    o Journal Entry, 30th October, 2021 --------- 14

III. Quips and Quotes -------------------------------- 15

    o Stealing from Shakespeare------------------ 16
    o Unfortunate Master ----------------------- 17
    o Alien ------------------------------------ 18
    o Listen ----------------------------------- 19
    o Riddle Me This --------------------------- 20
    o To Be Loved ------------------------------ 21
    o The Key ---------------------------------- 22
    o Trust ------------------------------------ 23
    o Insomnia --------------------------------- 24
    o Ode to Simplicity ------------------------ 25
    o Oh Darling, Only You --------------------- 26

IV. Verse and Valour ---------------------------------27

    o Carpe Diem ------------------------------- 28
    o Yes. The Poets are Melancholic ----------- 29
    o On Candles ------------------------------- 30
    o The Art of Travel ------------------------ 31
    o The Ache of an Artistic Soul ------------- 32
    o Sonny Boy -------------------------------- 33
    o Hail, Mother of the Earth and Heavens ------ 34
    o Imaginings from Childhood ----------------- 35
    o Oh! What a Mili-tree! --------------------- 36
    o Ode to a Reader -------------------------- 37
    o The Stars Found Her ---------------------- 38
    o Love Infinite ---------------------------- 39
    o is --------------------------------------- 40
    o A Dance with the Sunflowers -------------- 42

Early Works

A selection of verses I wrote from age 14 to 16 when I was largely inspired by the work of First and Second World War poets, writing many of my own poems on this theme. Though they lack technical merit, they were major stepping stones in my poetry journey and this collection could not be complete without them.

The Virtues

Faith is silent, strong and pure,
Bronze hair long and cheekbones sure,
Her features strong and dark eyes sharp,
Her laughter dancing like a harp.
Sweet but poignant, powerful,
Quiet, yet so beautiful,
Her voice akin to crashing seas,
Captivating, fierce and free.

Hope is filled with happy laughter,
Sweet things first, sad things after,
Golden locks curl round her face,
Her azure eyes aglow with grace.
Her crimson cheeks and mirthful mouth
Spread merriment from north to south,
And, friendly words, she'll find to say,
To any soul that comes her way.

Charity is soft and calm,
Smile, kind, and full of charm,
Her russet hair has natural curls
That waterfall in graceful swirls,
Her emerald eyes gleam lustrous light,
While pearly hands heal any plight,
And her gift to heal with whispered words,
Smiles over those who have heard.

BANG!

"BANG!" says the rifle in my ruby stained hand.
"BANG!" says the answer from over no man's land.
"BANG!" says the ground as, to ashes, she returns,
"BANG!" says the bullet as it takes my earthly turn.
"BANG!" says my body as it tangles in the wire,
"BANG!" says my head as I lie in pools of fire,
"BANG!" says my sight as I reach across to death,
"BANG!" says my heart as I free my final breath.

My Boy

I think of him, so small and white,
Wrapped up in a blanket, tight,
Circled in my warm embrace,
A peaceful smile on his face.

I think of him, so short and cute,
Standing proud in Papa's suit,
His curly mop and toothy grin
Stark against his freckled skin.

I think of him, so grown and tall,
Leaving on his way to school,
He pecks my cheek and turns away,
"Love you, Mam" I hear him say.

I think of him, so proud and keen,
Standing straight in olive green,
A restlessness I shall not quell;
His wish to serve his country well.

I think of him, out on his own,
His handsome face, now skin and
bone.
The fright of war and grief of
death
In every daring, nervous breath.

I think of him, so far away,
'Till finally there comes the day
The war is won, our freedom found;
And my precious babe is homeward
bound.

I see him stepping off the train,
His back is turned, I call his
name,
But as he turns around to me,
He is not the boy he used to be.

A haggard stare engulfs his face;
In both his cheeks, a hollow space.
Those wide blue eyes filled once
with light
Stir now with panic, pain and
fright.

And though he grins when I draw
near,
He holds himself with rigid fear,
And both the arms that circle me
Tremble unremittingly.

I think of decades gone and old,
The memories we felt unfold.
But the boy I raised in days gone
by
Is drowning, lost, in dying cries.

I gently clasp his weary form.
My tears rise cold and spill out
warm,
For I realise now, this man I hold
Is a broken one, with a broken
soul.

*Winning poem in the Never Such
Innocence- Bonus Strand "75"- poetry
competition in 2020*

6

The House on Mill Street Corner

The House on Mill Street Corner
With its panes of polished glass,
Was widely said to be a stead
Of fashionable class.
The straw thatch roof was golden,
The walls were painted white,
And the raven beams lain at the seams
Conceived a striking sight.
The host of this establishment
Was Mr John O. Comb,
Whose quiet smile and generous style
Was famous, like his home.
And all the people of the town
Would smile to hear him say,
"To witness human happiness
Would always make his day".
Then one bitter afternoon
In nineteen thirty-nine,
Mr Comb locked up that home
And left it far behind.
Both the people and the house
Watched him pack his bags and leave,
For tear-stained sand in no-man's land,
For bodies gone and grieved.
But the House on Mill Street corner
Still stood there, bold and strong.
So the townsfolk stayed, and laughed, and prayed
And sung Old John Comb's song.
They kept the straw thatch golden
And the walls were always white,
The buds were kept, the path was swept,
The windows gleaming bright.
The House on Mill Street Corner
Still the village work of art,
So they kept her home for John O. Comb,
And held her close at heart…

…But on the morrow of the fifth,
There came a dark distraction,
A tawny head and note that said
"John O. Comb, killed in action".
There was a silence in the street
Of which had never been before,
As each received, bowed, and grieved
The message at their door.
And later in the evening
When the sun was slowly dying
They heard a sound they later found
To be the poor house crying.
But the future was unmerciful
And as the moon rose higher,
A loud persistence in the distance
Said London was on fire.
The village cried as one for her,
They cried as one for John.
But still the fate that lay in wait
Was far from moving on.
For a cry, a crash, an outburst
And the sky turned wrathful red.
A stray bomb fell; a scene from Hell,
And in the heart, a dread.
A piercing scream of agony,
A shard of raven beam,
A being drained, a presence waned,
A vision torn along the seam.
And then the fire flared no more,
A glaring ember slithered down.
A dying groan; a silence, known,
Crept around the little town.
And when a burst of feeble sunlight
Poked out behind the hill,
It sadly peered where flames had seared
And left a wound too deep to fill.
But at last, the town was quiet,
Save for apprehensive throbs
Of nervous feet along the street
And quiet muffled sobs.
And when the people saw the carcass,
It broke them, and they mourned her,
For a raven frame was all that remained
Of the House on Mill Street corner.

Prose and Posies

These small paragraphs of prose come from my daydreams and imaginings. Pieced together in the rambling manner of my thoughts, they leave more room for questions than answers.

Outcast

Outcast. It's an interesting word, isn't it? It feels empty
and scratched, slipping off your tongue and leaving you
unsatisfied with the result. It's not like 'belonging', which
tastes warm against your lips, or 'fellowship', which rolls from
your throat with the whisper of fulfilment. No, 'outcast' is
reminiscent of tortured breaths, of empty dread, of terrible
silence. It casts a vision of damp walls with sprawling moss, blue
tipped fingers grasped together, cracked nails printing crescents
into flesh. Tangled hair hanging around hollowed cheeks, permanent
tears glistening on fluttering lashes, lips split and decorated
with rivers of red. It paints a picture of desolation, of
uncertainty; of the terrible dread that drifts in on the tide of
unknowing.

Maybe it is an interesting word because it has undefinable
meaning; because it's a word for everybody; or because it's a word
for nobody; or because it's a word for everything; or because it's
a word for nothing. Because it means all of that or none of that,
and is a word that will remain nothing more or nothing less than
exactly what it is. It's a word that tells the story of someone
who has been forgotten by the world, or someone who forgot the
world, or someone who is remembered badly by the world, or someone
who remembers the world badly. And some people live by it because
of things that are their fault, or aren't their fault, or are
someone else's fault, or are nobody's fault. Because they look
different, speak differently, smile differently, think
differently, believe differently, or because they merely act
differently.

And yet, what is the true definition of 'outcast'? If it means
someone who does not fit in, then are we not all outcasts? We are
not the same. We fit in with each other because we do not fit in
with each other. Because we are humans, and humans cannot be the
same. Because we have individual souls, individual minds,
individual hearts and individual natures. Because we are

9

individuals, and there can only be outcasts in the world if
everyone in the world is an outcast.

What Life Can Be

What can life be? Can it be the nostalgic scent of rain on warm tarmac? The sight of glittering sunbeams dancing merrily across an autumn spinney? The bubbling mirth of an evening with dear company? Is it even the cold hand of death as it steals the souls of those beloved? Perhaps life is waking before dawn and watching the ancient star stretch her dazzling fingers across an English countryside, dusting meadows with whispers of light. It is the canvas of an evening sky, each different from the last as God allows painters of old to work magic across that celestial easel. It is the bittersweet woe of antiquated books, dusty pages breathing scents of time-sweetened stories, curled ink weaving through tales of lost romance. It is the mischievous echo of an empty hall, soft, pattering footfalls dancing like a chorus of blithe fairies. It is the delicate perfume of a springtime noon, elegant roses dropping petals into blankets of rainbow fragrance, chirpy songbirds chanting their cunning songs across stretches of azure sky. Life is all these moments in time, these fragments of memory. It is the vibrant myriad of emotions and thoughts and experiences and dreams, bound together by the spirit of a human soul. That, perhaps, is what life can be.

Quite Beautiful

   I had been sitting on mounds of delicate moss in the shade of
a smiling tree, trailing my hand in the glassy pond-water beside
my knee and peering over the side. My reflection had stared back.
It rippled and swirled and shimmered, and I was nothing but ugly.
But the wind had danced through leafy boughs above my bowed head,
swept a bundle of fluttering emeralds from their speckled perch
and settled them in sweet formation around the mirage of my
rippling reflection. Crowned with nature's finest gems, I looked
back at myself. The tree looked. The clouds looked. The birds
looked. Even the crickets paused their busy chatter and looked. It
was a strange moment. I felt the shape of a crown floating above
my tawny hair. The air shimmered in the heat, and a warm hand
gently wiped the tears from my eyes. Love, unfathomable love,
filled my soul. Love for who I was and in Whose image I am made.
When I met my own gaze again, I did not, could not, look ugly
anymore. In fact, as I watched the halo dance about my head in the
June scented breeze, I had come to realise that, maybe, I looked
quite beautiful.

Daydreamer

She is a soul that lives in a land of spiralling letters and
sun-drenched daisies, dancing dew drops in secret meadows and
fragrant drapes of honeysuckle. Wild tangles of woodland trails
and sun-laden glades are refuge to her wandering heart, and she
travels further, deeper, longer, into the safety of this haven.
Her palace lies in the heart of this breathing forest, framed with
overgrown ivy and sparkling streams. There is life in every
corner- empty ballrooms reminiscent of gatherings from the gods;
the softest echo of laughter. Lively raindrops glancing off
crystal window panes, flashes of sunlight on over used teacups.
The kitchen grate smokes merrily and the kettle whistles in time
as drying flowers twinkle prettily from ceiling rafters.

When dusk falls and the stars poke out from veils of velvet
cloud, crickets hum, bats fly, and the moon begins her gentle
reign over the glowing earth. Barefoot and wrapped in floating
layers of silk, she dances over dew tipped grass to the music of
midnight hours, lost in a reverie of enchantment and delight. When
winter's freezing fingers trail across her skin, she darts back
into the haven of her home and snuggles into handknit jumpers,
frayed and patched and lived in.

She wakes the kettle for a steaming cup of tea and curls up
on familiar sofa cushions, listening to rain patter outside the
window. Moonlight glows delicately in shadowed corners,
ink-stained quills and crumpled paper decorating the desk as
fireflies dance in the light of her eyes, and glimmer in the
hearth. Sleep, the only creature to persistently evade her
inviting smile, creeps in solely during these bewitching hours and
allows her to follow him towards the land of his kin. Dawn
awakens, birds sing, and she breathes gently to the rhythm of
happiness.

A dream and nothing more.

Journal Entry, 30th October 2021

There was such a beautiful sunset tonight. Warm, blazing orange woven with teal blue thread; indigo melting into rosy rouge. The sky had been laid bare, a canvas for the majestic hand of God, and He had painted with the awe-inspiring magic of which only He may yield. What happiness such beauty invokes!

Quips and Quotes

As short and sweet as the title, these pieces rarely go beyond a few lines and are little snippets of poetry that occasionally swim before me in the great pool of my imagination.

Stealing from Shakespeare

To believe or not to believe, that is the question.

                              -Not Hamlet, maybe St. Peter

Unfortunate Master

The art of being misunderstood is one I have been unfortunate
enough to master.

Alien

I sometimes think I was born in the wrong world.
A world too ugly,
Or too beautiful,
Or maybe a world too lonely
For souls like mine.

Listen

In my heart I hear a thought one thousand ways.
The one that leaves my lilting lips stays.
The rest will fall forever still and fade.

Riddle Me This

Tell me,
If we are merely a clump of meaningless cells
Living meaningless lives,
With meaningless dreams,
How do we know
What its means to
Hope?

To Be Loved

People may reject the presence of God because they doubt their own
self-worth.
But I love to think that
He made the flaming sun, the glowing moon,
Budding cherry blossoms, mountains of majesty,
And oceans of unknowable depth,
And yet still thought
He needed you.

The Key

I have a theory that if we did nothing
But smile at the sun,
Laugh with our neighbours,
Ramble through ancient forests,
And eat too many strawberries,
Happiness would be a permanent resident in our hearts.

Trust

When the waves come in
And fill your nose and ears and eyes
With salty blue,
Reach out.
My hand will be waiting for you.

                    -Jesus

Insomnia

Hail the day, my eyes do not close!
My mind re-awoke when the moon re-arose,
And why must it be, when sleep does call my name,
That the stars have gone out and there's sunlight again?

An Ode to Simplicity

I have drowned in deathly depths of dormant deserts,
And soared the seven sunless souls of sea,
I have mourned for mountains made from mad and melancholy minds,
But rejoiced with royal riches when the rain remembered me.

Oh Darling, Only You

Trace a trail of sunbeams from the tangle of my veins,
Craft a crown of iron from the ashes of my chains,
Unwind the web of brambles built about my bleeding heart,
Oh darling, only you, my love, may tear my soul apart.

Verse and Valour

*Written from flashes of inspiration that have me feeling nothing
but the poetry coursing through my veins, these verses are among my
most valued works in the collection. My blood, sweat, tears and soul
lie here- tread with caution.*

Carpe Diem

Oh Captain, my Captain,
My pillar of heat and comfort,
My refuge in the storm of servitude,
Advocate of my soul, speaker of my wistful heart,
Come hither to my wandering land of passions
To the withering hand of my feeble pen,
To the untamed beast of my spirit,
A creature whose wingless flight and cry of anguish
Creates the shadow of a monster.
Not a monster of wrathful vengeance or grotesque shapes,
Of evil whispers or growls of seething hate,
But one of desperate whimpers and glowing eyes,
Of fleeting heartbeats and tangles of silver mane.
A monster created from scrabbling thoughts running through
My veins,
And delicate hopes not yet crushed by
Harsh realities of the seen world.
And the cry of this magnificent,
Ugly,
Yearning creature,
Is something heard only by those
With beasts of their own;
By those whose spirit forms a monster's shadow,
A monster's blood,
A monster's bone.
Something understood only by the
Likeness of my kind,
And
The likeness of my soul.
By the gathering of us,
Of dreamers.
By the gathering of
Dying poets
And
Their believers.

Yes. The Poets are Melancholic.

People laugh at the poets and call them
Sad,
Hopeless,
Or pathetic .
And people will always think this
Although it is a thought untrue.
And maybe the poets are melancholic,
But not because they are sad,
Hopeless,
or pathetic.
But because they do not see the world like most do.
They see a little too much, a little too deep for most people to
ever understand.
Maybe the poets are melancholic
Because they can see the fleeting flicker of something more in
every vibrant sunset,
And the promise of something infinite in every dying flower.
They see the the beauty of earthly things
And feel a yearning ache,
A burning throb,
From knowing this must merely be a glimpse
Of something limitless.
From knowing that this wonder and magnificence they see before
them
Will soon die, like every other mortal thing.
So the poets are melancholic
Because the everlasting beauty for which they search so earnestly,
Will only find them when the flaming hand of death
Reaches out towards their sleeping form,
And guides them to a sun-laden palace
And gates of glaring pearl.
The poets are melancholic
Because they know they must wait alone in this dying world
Until their turn,
With only the promise of such beauty,
Such glory,
Such majesty,
To keep them alive.

On Candles

We are like candles.
Quiet. Peaceful. Ambient.
Mood setters, perhaps,
Or things people don't realise they
need
Until they lose one.

We become light for these souls.
For trembling children scared of
shadows and
Skeletal hands under the bed.
For youthful writers of avid zeal,
feverish pencil scratches
Illuminated by our amber glow.
For dozing dreamers curled on
window seats, tracing trails of
delicate rain with ghostly fingers.
For gentle readers, squinting their
tired eyes at tales of woven ink
and flickering flames.
Light.
For the people who need us.
But as we shine like this,
Winking brightly in the darkened
room.
We grow smaller.
Fade.
Sacrificed.
For those around us.
And the stronger we shine
The faster we shrink,
A terrifying paradox
Of unsettling
dread,
A painful piece of
Tangible prose,
The threat of an eruption
Where our differences
Will ignite.

For where I burn.
And burn.
And burn.
And burn
And get left behind because I am
never quite remembered
Or thought of for
Any reason
Beyond what I do for someone else,

Flickering,
Unnoticed and forgotten on a dusty
shelf.
Wax pooling from my eyes and
sliding into a sea of mountains.
Sinking softly
Patiently,
Fatefully,
Into nothing.
One sad, final teardrop before my
light is quietly
Dimmed.
To shine, nevermore.

For where I fade like this, into
the land of lost forevers,
You tip.
Over the shelf.
In a cloud of burning dust.
You land on the wooden boards
And your tiny fire latches
stubbornly on.
Tendrils of smoke and acrid scents.
Your pain at being forgotten
becomes anguish,
And anguish becomes rage,
And rage reaches flaming tentacles
of glowing wrath along the
Cracks in the floor.
And you erupt
In a blazing shape of agony.
Burning.
Burning.
Burning.
Until you have destroyed so much
that there is nothing left to
destroy
But yourself.
And you cannot help but wonder
As you join the faceless ashes
around you with a final,
Broken,
Sigh,
What might have happened
Had they
Just remembered
To look
For
Us

The Art of Travel

When I stand under the sunless sky, bathing in the starlight of
galaxies forever unsearched,
I am the rhythm of the pounding waves around me.
I am the magnetic pull of every drenching heave, every falling
droplet.
I am the sand sticking to my shivering shins, the fragrant breeze
combing salt into my glinting locks.
I am the tear drops and sea drops which run entwined down my burnt
cheeks, hot from the old sun or the new night or the everlasting
ache of constant knowing and unknowing.

I am every place I have ever been and
I will be every place I have yet to see,
And for everywhere I pause on these dauntless travels,
I take the pieces of my soul for which I search, leaving, in
return,
Fragments of my untamed spirit, forever immortalised in memory I
silently steal.

The Ache of an Artistic Soul

It is a strange thing to have an artist's eyes
But not an artist's hand.
To paint an ocean sunrise on my eyelids
But have no skill to sketch the sand.

It is like torture from a place so heavenly
That I welcome the searing lurch
Of my heart, as it sees the unknown masterpieces hidden
Where no soul but mine can search.

It is a strange thing then,
And a sad one, as it be,
That this gallery of wonders I can capture with my heart,
Will never have a place amongst our feet.

But is tangled in the stars
And drowned in the sea.
And trodden beneath the steps of those
Whose soul may never be set free

Sonny Boy

Across a maddened mouth of mud
And blood and sickened cries,
Sunk in graves where whence they fell,
There, someone's son shall die.

Through a crown of ashen clouds
A grey winged hero flies.
A failing trail of valour true,
There, someone's son shall die.

Beneath the foam of mermaid's breath
Where flippant sea-gods lie,
From silver heat and sunken ship,
There, someone's son shall die.

Alone he'll be on a red-tipped ridge
Stars shivering in the sky,
Eyes aflame with bullet rain,
And someone's son shall die.

Hail, Mother of the Earth and Heavens

Lady of the sun
With her veil of
Burnished gold.

Lady of the moon
With tears of
Silver stories untold.

Lady of the stars
Who glistens bright
Under her shroud of grace.

Lady of the sky
Who cradles the world
In her azure embrace.

Imaginings from Childhood

'Twas the echo of a robin-bird, that key to Crimson Crest,
Aflame with ancient feathers and a whistle in his breast,

And yet, he'd sit with regal gravity, a prince amidst his land,
Providing for his subjects with a simple turn of hand.

He'd perform his duty merrily, a-warbling away,
But he'd rest with royal fervour in a glorious array.

I would watch him whilst he slumbered and I heard him whilst he
worked,
He was nothing but enchanting; in his duty, never shirked.

He was both a robin red-breast and a prince with pride of place,
He could sing with softened sweetness yet reside with royal grace,

Thus, he may be naught but antiquated iron in the end,
But he'll always be my robin-bird, my prince, my dearest friend.

Poet's note:

*Whether it's a riddle, a metaphor, a series of puns, this poem
represents the childish fascination directed towards a great,
wrought iron key used to unlock the house. With its rusty exterior,
the child beholds it as Grand Prince of the Robin-birds, and
remembers it with child-like adoration.*

Oh! What a Mili-tree!

"Oh! If there could be an army!" One day, says I to thee,
"And if we were to draft it from the different English trees-

We would have a host of bowman from the birches by the bay,
With their supple, bending boughs and their nimble, neat array.

The pines would be essential; they are armed abundantly,
And their winter-long persistence would perfect our infan-tree.

The cavalry, however, may present us some distress,
Although I think the great horse chestnuts would be apt to serve
us best.

And look! You see that cedar tree alone beside the stream?
From him we'd gain a Chaplain to uplift the team's esteem.

Then that little copse of sycamores could be our aviation,
Whilst the weeping willows yonder would provide a medic station.

And lastly, what's an army if it lacks a general's hold?
So an oak tree with its majesty would be the best enrolled.

Oh! Imagine what a force we'd have!" That day, says I to thee-
"A marvellous amusement and the truest mili-tree!"

   Poets note:

The trees for each military role have been chosen with care:
1. The slender appearance of a Birch reminds me of an elegant
bowman.
2. Pine trees endure through all weather and seasons, thus they seem
to work best as the infantry.
3. Horse chestnuts = cavalry... what more need I say.
4. It was supposedly Cedar wood upon which Christ was crucified.
Such a tree would be perfect for a Chaplain.
5. Sycamores have little "helicopter" seeds, so I just had to put
them as the air force.
6. Weeping willows have healing properties, and I felt their
sheltered canopy could represent a medic's tent.
7. Oak trees are just so stately and majestic, no other tree would
do for a general!

Ode to a Reader

He has elegant hands of burnished gold and burnt sienna curls,
His eyes are flickering candle lights, his smile of argent pearls,
He holds a soft expression on the hard lines of his face
And each imperfect feature rests perfectly in place.

He lightly clasps my fingers with the whisper of a kiss;
Escorts me down corridors, my hand braided through his.
And we dance in starlit ballrooms to the music of the moon,
Afloat with pooling silver and her distant, haunting tune.

He snares my soulful dreaming like the ghostly hand of death,
Holds grace in every movement and my heart in every breath.
And time belongs to no one as we twirl towards the dawn,
Watch the golden sun rays melt the diamonds on the lawn,

I am a daring dreamer and he is my daring dream
I make his mirage tangible, weave life in every seam
And grey though my reality when break of day draws nigh
Sweeter is the heartache of a love who never dies.

The Stars Found Her

When they come to fetch me tell them I have gone astray.
Led by limbs of laurel trees and eyes of weeping willow leaves,
And bones of birch and silver eaves,
And stars, in sweet array.

When they come to fetch me tell them I have wandered far,
Through ribs of ripened river beds and hearts of rushing ocean
heads,
And lips of falling water threads,
And summons of a star.

When they come to fetch me tell them I have fallen deep,
In hands of harrowed hurricanes and brows of breaching battle
rains,
And veins of vibrant crystal-panes,
And stars of idle sleep.

And when they came to fetch me I was drifting, ever lost,
In frays of frantic fairy flight and drops of molten candlelight
And gowns of effervescent white,
And stars of flaming frost…

…And though I now lie six feet 'neath
The daffodils of yesterday,
The stars, with luring laugh
Claim now my roaming soul,
No more astray.

Love Infinite

It is so easy to fall in love.
With musical sunsets,
And the smell of weathered
books.
Wind through meadow-grass,
Babbling brooks.
Perfumed roses,
Sunlight through leaves,
Iced coffee,
Cobbled streets,
The daintiest web a spider
weaves.

That pencil with the perfect
point,
Or,
The best spoon in the cutlery
drawer,
Or,
The honeycomb in your eyes
when a sunbeam dances across
the floor.

And cinnamon sticks,
Hot tea,
A fluttering butterfly,
flitting round the tree,
Moonlight,
Morning glow,
The crunch of forget-me-nots
in brown paper,
And the moment your sunflower
begins to grow.

Oh, it is so easy to fall in
love!
With ink scratches,
And candlelight,
And raw, hearty laughter,
And turtle doves cooing in the
rafters,
And the smell of rain left
behind after,
A hot, August night.

And I could walk the earth
forever,
Loving every seed, every
petal, every flower,
Every crack in the pavement
where dandelions sleep,
And roots of that willow reach
deep,
Under the lake it embraces,
Weeping for all the faces,
It has watched through the
ages:
Young lovers,
Old widows,
Sweet mothers,
And mages
Of mythical legends and tales
of wagers
Against ancient dragons from
stories I love and read,
Under the shadows of water
reeds,
And dragonflies, green.

Oh, how I love all this,
Which my eyes may see
And know the sight of beauty,
And my ears may hear
And know the sound of sheer
Delight-
And my heart,
It knows! Oh it knows how to
be torn apart
And stitched together
With golden thread of purple
heather,
And all the love with which
this loving world may part.
Love,
Oh love,
Infinite.

is

I will
smile
with my
soul.
With life that
exists
only in
me.
My heart will
fill with fervour,
faith
and fear
in
the blink
of an eye,
and I will show you
life is
beautiful.

I will fall
into the
dusty pages of
old books
with
broken spines
and stories of
myths long
forgotten.
Entangled in
romance
I will
wonder
at the tales
woven through
tired fingers
and
brilliant minds.
And sometimes
I will let my
tears fall
down
on pages
not remembered by
the
world.

And I will dance like a fire,
Wild passion.
Crackling energy.

Sparks
Flying through the
air from
my feet as
they glide along.
And then it will die.
And I will
softly float like
embers.
And ash.
As it
Sprinkles
down to
dust.

Sometimes I will cry
and tears will fall
from my eyes
And glisten on lashes,
lowered.
They will
slide
down cheekbones
burnt bronze in
the sun,
And it will be
pained,
But beautiful.
And yet sometimes I
will scream,
eyes swollen.
Red.
Mouth tangled
in a terrible grimace
as demons torment
me inside the
cavern of my
crusading soul.
Salt
tracks down my
cheeks.
Tears dripping,
sliding,
off my chin.
Landing in the sea of
anguish
at my
feet.

But
Sometimes I will
laugh.
And the sound will echo
around,
tinkle,
like sun rays
on a crystal stream.
Or it will bubble
like
squirrels
tittering in
leafy boughs,
rarely heard
But softly sweet.
Or
it will bellow,
loud and clear,
thunderous and honest.
True.
Like ancient trees
of fantastical myth
and churning
seas of mirth.

And
Sometimes
I will quietly
listen
and love
the music of
sunrise.
Meadows twinkling with
dew,
a million
tiny
diamonds
of every colour
in the
rainbow and
more.
And the bird-song
will sound like
a thousand angels
laughing in
melodious harmony.
A chorus
Of heavenly chords.
And I will shine.
glow.
When the sun spills
shimmering gold
on my lips

and eyelids,
and I breathe
the scent of daisies.
Forget-me-nots.
Sunflowers.
As the breeze
blows perfumes
of Eden
through my mind,
clearing
the cobwebs
and smiling
on
Me.

And
one day,
in the pages
of
future
moments,
in the majestic
timelapse of
years
to come.
In the unknowable
nothing of
fate or
destiny,
chance or
Divine intention.
Someone will find
me in
the depths of my
enchanted view
of life,
and
will love me
Wholly.
Entirely.
Willingly.
Just as I
am.
And
they will love
the
world I fell
in love
with
just
as it
is.

A Dance with the Sunflowers

Golden heads gaze,
At sunbeams ablaze,
Through rivers of leaf and light.
And the day melts away,
To song of the fae,
As I search for my soul in the night.
As I search for my soul in the nectar of night,
As I search for my soul in the night.

Golden eyes glare,
At Cupid's affair,
With Wind in the valley of thorn.
And the taste of her breath,
Stirs roses in death,
As I search for my soul in the dawn.
As I search for my soul in the blossom of dawn,
As I search for my soul in the dawn.

Golden lips part,
At whispers of heart,
From caverns that shiver and sigh.
And the calling of fate,
Forever must wait,
As I search for my soul in the sky.
As I search for my soul in the vennels of sky,
As I search for my soul in the sky.

Golden cheeks glow,
As sunflowers grow,
From heavens of promises, free.
And the waltz of His wraith,
Leaves nothing but faith,
As I search for my soul in the sea.
As I search for my soul in the raptures of sea,
As I search for my soul in the sea.

Printed in Great Britain
by Amazon